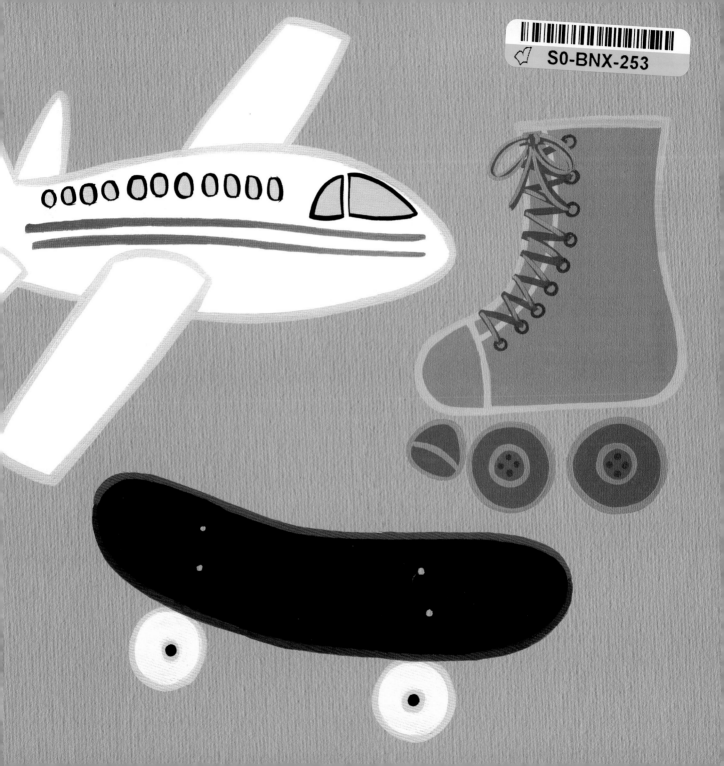

Designed by Flowerpot Press in Franklin, TN.
www.FlowerpotPress.com
Designer: Jonas Fearon Bell
Editor: Katrine Crow
ROR-0808-0108
ISBN: 978-1-4867-1262-5
Made in China/Fabriqué en Chine

Things That Go...

Illustrated by Lisa M Gardiner

Something that goes FAST is a CAR.

(Some cars go *REALLY* fast!)

Something that goes SLOW is a TRICYCLE.

(Or maybe they go fast?)

Something that goes UP
is a ROCKET.

(Later it goes down.)

Something that goes
ON WATER
is a SAILBOAT.

(Water and wind and away you go!)

Something that goes IN THE AIR is an AIRPLANE.

(Sometimes it goes on the ground, too.)

Something that goes *ON YOUR FEET* is a ROLLER SKATE.

(They work best when you have two.)

Something that goes *WITH* YOUR FEET is a BIKE.

(Just don't wear your roller skates.)

Something that goes ON FOUR *LEGS* is a HORSE.

(What else goes on four legs?)

Something that goes ON FOUR *WHEELS* is a SKATEBOARD.

(What else goes on four wheels?)

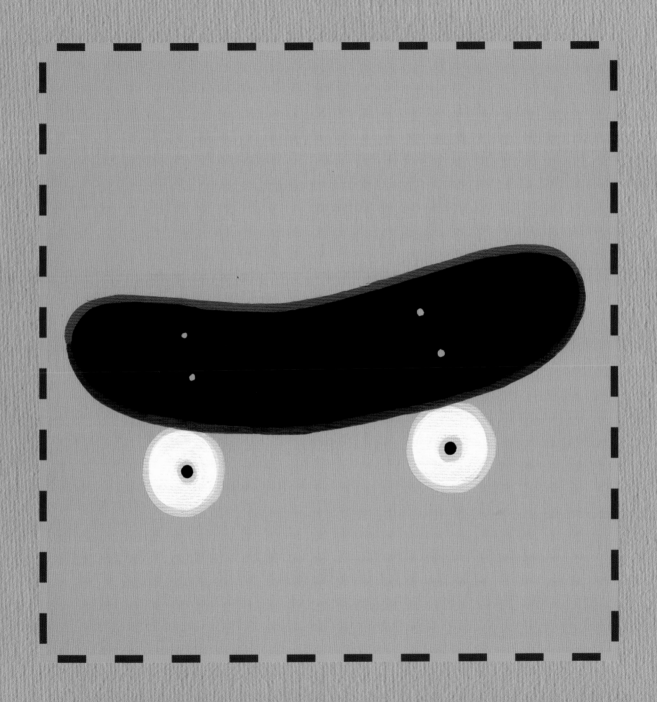

Something that goes
WHERE THE
WIND BLOWS
is a
HOT AIR BALLOON.

(Up, up, and away!)